# Sirius the Seagull

## A Story of Family, Travel, and Love

Grandma Lulu

# Table of Contents

# Dedication

I dedicate this book to my granddaughter, Amara, as a source of inspiration, and to Jason for supporting my creativity and dreams.

this page is just for corresponding illustrations

the text will be remove while publishing

S

# Chapter 1:
# How I Got a Family

"Hi! My name is Sirius and I'm a seagull!" chirped excitedly. Let me tell you how my mom found me-and how I came to life.

After a few long days working in the states of Idaho and Wyoming, my Mom decided to enjoy the amazing landscape that Grand Teton National Park has to offer. Grand Teton is the highest mountain in the park at 13,775 feet tall. In simpler words: it's huge! This park is filled with beautiful hiking trails, diverse wildlife, vibrant flowers, sparkling lakes, and breathtaking mountain views.

She picked a pair of earrings shaped like bear footprints. Then she looked up and saw me. I was sitting on a store shelf-a little toy seagull. She took a deep breath and skipped a heartbeat. Something told her I was special. She whispered, with wonder in her voice, "I think I know where you belong."

WYOMING
COLORAD
AUSTRALIA

Then she smiled and said softly, "There is someone from the East Coast-he's from Baltimore. He loves the sea and marine life. I think he'll adopt you". She bought me and gently tucked me inside her purse. The next morning, we boarded an airplane and flew to Denver.

S

When we got to her home, a man was waiting there. She handed me to him like a special gift. "I saw this seagull and thought of you," she told him. "Since you both love the ocean, I felt like you should be together." He looked at me curiously. No one had ever given him a seagull before. He took his time picking a name and finally called me Sirius. And that's when I came alive. Now I call them Mom and Dad. And that's how I became part of this family.

One snail... two snails...
three snails...

I said, "It's time for bed now. I'm going to count snails until I fall asleep." As I snuggled into the bed, I added, "Good night, Mom and Dad." They answered together, smiling, "Good night, Sirius." Mom tucked me in with a warm blanket. I whispered, "One snail... two snails... three snails..."

If you could adopt any animal as a pet, what would it be? What would you name it?

# Chapter 2: The Tidy Home

One day, Mom—the one who picked me from the shelf—came home and found a big mess in my room. She opened her eyes wide. “Sirius, Sirius, Sirius! What have you done?” I looked up and asked, “Are you mad, Mommy?” She took a breath and said gently, “No, but I don’t like how the room looks. We need to set some rules.” I asked, tilting my head, “Rules?” Mom explained, “Rules help us live better together. Like when you play with friends—sharing toys and being kind are rules too. And in our house, everyone helps keep it clean and cozy. I’ll show you where things go when you’re done using them.”

S

She showed me how to use the hamper for dirty clothes. So, I put mine in there. Next, we picked up my toys and placed them in boxes and on shelves. "I'll do it myself next time!" I promised her. I fixed the bed covers and threw the trash in the bin. Mom smiled and said, "Good job! High three!"

Then she started singing a funny song that sounded like

*We Are the Champions by Queen*: "

♫*Sirius is the champion,*

*Sirius is the champion,*

*Sirius is the champion...*

*of the world!*"♫

Daddy peeked in and laughed. "Okay, Freddie Mercury, what's all this about?" Mom grinned and told him I had cleaned my room all by myself. Dad gave me a high three too! Soon, it was 8 o'clock, and I was getting sleepy. Dad said, "Good night, Buddy!" Mom said, "Good night, Sirius!" I whispered back, "Good night!" Daddy tucked me in, and I started counting fish. "One fish... two fish... three fish..." Before I knew it, I was fast asleep.

BEDTIME
WASH HANDS
BE KIND
HELP EACH OTHER
READ

What rules do you follow at home?
Can you think of a new one that would help your family?

S

# Chapter 3: Uncle Larry

We have a great routine on weekdays, but I love the weekends. That's when Mom and Dad are around all day— we play, go on adventures, and tell stories about what happened during the week. It was a beautiful, sunny spring day—perfect for the outdoors. Mom picked a trail in Golden, Colorado, and Daddy drove us there for a bicycle ride. As we biked along the trail, we passed people walking. I told everyone we saw,

"Hi! I'm Sirius and I'm a seagull!"

They always smiled and said hi back.

After a while, we stopped to rest, drink water, and eat snacks. I wandered off the trail, curious about something. Daddy gently walked me back. He said in a concerned voice, "Sirius, Sirius, Sirius... It's not safe to leave the trail. The ground can be uneven or dangerous. And we also want to protect plants and animals that live here."

I asked, “Protect what, Daddy?” “Well,” he explained, “like the monarch butterfly. People who study them know what flowers they like. If we walk too close or crush them, the butterflies won’t feel safe to make a home.” He looked around the meadow. “That special place they live in—the flowers, the plants—that’s called a habitat.”

S

I asked,
"Is a habitat like their home?"
"Yes," Daddy nodded.
"A habitat is a natural home for animals, plants, or bugs."
I nodded back.
"Okay, I won't leave the trail anymore. I want to be safe and protect the habitats around me."
Daddy smiled widely.
"Excellent, Sirius! Give me a high three!"
And all three of us slapped hands and flippers in the air—
High three!

S

I looked around and saw so many shades of green and brown. Tiny wildflowers peeked out near the riverbank. Big rocks piled into mountains, showing the cliffs where water had once flowed. The evergreen trees reached high into the sky, and other trees were starting to bloom for spring. We shared fruit and snacks, cleaned up after ourselves, and then headed home. Back home, we put away our bikes, helmets, and backpacks.

After a hot shower and yummy dinner, we curled up to watch a movie. And you won't believe what happened next... The movie showed a scene in San Francisco! Every time the Golden Gate Bridge came on screen, we all shouted: "Cisco!" Then a beautiful seagull flew across the bay. I screamed, "Uncle Larry! Uncle Larry! That's my famous uncle! He's in movies! He lives in Los Angeles, where they shoot a lot of them!" Daddy's eyes went wide. "Wow! I didn't know. Awesome!" Mom said, "That's awesome, Sirius! I can totally see the resemblance."

After the movie, they tucked me into bed. While I was counting shrimp, Mom sang something funny to Daddy, to the tune of *More Than a Woman by the Bee Gees*:

♫ *"More than a Booster...*
*You are the Booster to me!"* ♫

Daddy chuckled.

"Okay, Bee Gees, time for bed."

Before they left, I asked, "Daddy, why did Mommy call you a Booster?" He smiled and said, "That's a story for another day."

What's your favorite place to explore in nature?

S

# Chapter 4:
# Sirius Goes to Seattle

We were driving to the airport while Mommy started singing something similar to the song

*Don't Stop Believin' by Journey...*

*♫ "She was a small-town girl,*
*Recently moved there.*
*She took the airplane and moved to Denver.*
*He was a silly boy,*
*That came from Baltimore,*
*He took a flight and stayed in Denver, too." ♫*

Sirius asked, "Mom, what is that story you are singing?" Mom said, "This is the story of how Mom and Daddy met."

S

She explained, "Daddy used to live in Baltimore, and I used to live in Puerto Rico. We both moved to Colorado at the end of 2019. In March 2020, the world went into lockdown because of a new infection that was affecting everyone. During the summer of 2021, I met your Dad at the bowling alley. It was a Saturday afternoon. We played twice and had a great time. He drove me back to my car. He asked me to wait-because he wanted to give me a hug.

I waited, and he kissed me, and hugged me... and that was our first kiss."

Sirius said, "Awww!"

Daddy (mocking) said, "That's not exactly how it happened." Sirius curiously asked, "Then what happened?"

Daddy replied, "I'll tell you another day." We flew on an airplane and arrived in Seattle. We drove to the apartment where we were staying, rested for a few minutes, and organized our luggage. Soon after, we got ready to explore the city.

PIKE PLACE
FISH MARKET
S

# Seattle Day 1

First, we walked to the famous Pike Place Market. It's a six-story building filled with vendors, food, flowers, arts, and crafts. There are long lines of crates full of fruits and vegetables, some restaurants, and the attraction of the day- the fishmongers throwing fish in the air and catching them before putting them on display! It's a noisy place. They receive approximately 10,000 visitors daily.
Can you imagine?

We had lunch at the iconic first Starbucks store. They have a lot of food-and of course, coffee. I didn't drink coffee. Mommy thinks it might not suit me well.

S
L

Since we were looking for the best views in the city, we went to Kerry Park. From there, we walked to Queen Anne's Park. We saw beautiful views, vibrant flowers, and tulips dancing under the sun all day. We finished our walk near the harbor, enjoying a fresh breeze on our faces. After sunset, we came back and rested. Uncle Larry came to visit and stayed with us overnight I was exhausted and started counting blueberries...

"One blueberry, two blueberries, three blueberries..." .

# Seattle – Day 2

The next morning, we had fruit and oatmeal for breakfast with Uncle Larry. He was flying back to Los Angeles to work on a new movie. He would be the main seagull character in the film!

Sirius said, "Goodbye, Uncle Larry. Thank you for visiting us. I love you!"

Uncle Larry said, "I love you, too, little Sirius. Come visit me in Los Angeles anytime."

Mom and Dad hugged him and thanked him for visiting. Mom said, "We enjoyed having you around. Visit us anytime."

Dad added, "Have a safe trip. Good luck on the movie!"

It was a beautiful sunny day, and we headed to the Space Needle. It has the first all-glass outdoor elevator in North America. Imagine going up while seeing everything outside! From the top, we saw downtown, Mount Rainier, and many other panoramic views. We also walked across glass floors and looked down at the city below.

We visited the Chihuly Garden and Glass. The artist used amazing colors to create huge glass figures. Some were so big, they could only fit in a house if we removed all the walls and furniture! Next, we went to the Seattle Public Library. It's a large building with many fun things to do. We walked around quietly and wrote down a few book titles to read later. We came back to the apartment to get ready to visit an island. Sirius asked, "Daddy, what's taking so long? I want to see the island!" Daddy said, "Easy, Sirius. I want to be prepared." Sirius asked, "What are you preparing?"

Daddy replied, "Snacks, water, a windbreaker, sunblock, and a few other things." My favorite part was visiting Bainbridge Island-and seeing Uncle Larry, of course! To get there, we took a ferry. For half an hour, we saw Seattle getting smaller and smaller. Bainbridge Island is a small, picturesque town with trees, flowers, and birds everywhere. I was so happy to see other birds around me. With the sea so close, we felt a great breeze. People were kayaking, sailing, and walking-just like us-as they explored the shoreline. Sirius shouted, "Hi! I'm Sirius and I'm a seagull!" Everyone said hi back. We passed small shops and restaurants. After a great lunch, the weather turned cloudy and windy. As we walked back to the ferry, a storm hit.

S

It was suddenly dark, cold, and scary. The wind howled, and rain poured down fast. Mommy wrapped her hands around me, and Daddy stretched his big coat to shield us both. On the return boat ride, we watched Seattle getting closer and the storm drifting away behind us. When we got home safely, we packed our bags for the trip back the next day. Sirius said, "Mom, Dad, thank you for this vacation."

"You're welcome. I loved sharing this adventure with you." She kissed me on the head. Dad said, "Me too. I'm glad we had this time together."

Sirius whispered,

“Dad, now I understand why it’s important to be prepared. Sorry for being impatient.”

Daddy grinned.

“That’s okay. I’m just glad we’re safe. Give me a Hi-three!”

And together we all slapped a big, happy Hi-three!

Mom started singing
something similar to
*"Don't Cry for Me Argentina"*
*from Evita.*
*"Don't cry for me, Colorado,*
♫ *The truth is, I never left you,*
*I was on vacation,*
*And now I'm*
*coming back...".* ♫
Daddy said, "
Come to bed, Evita."
"One oyster,
two oysters, three oysters..."
And soon after,
I was asleep.

Sirius felt scared during the storm, but his parents protected him and helped him feel safe. Can you think of a time when you felt scared, and someone helped you feel better? What did they do that made you feel safe or happy again?

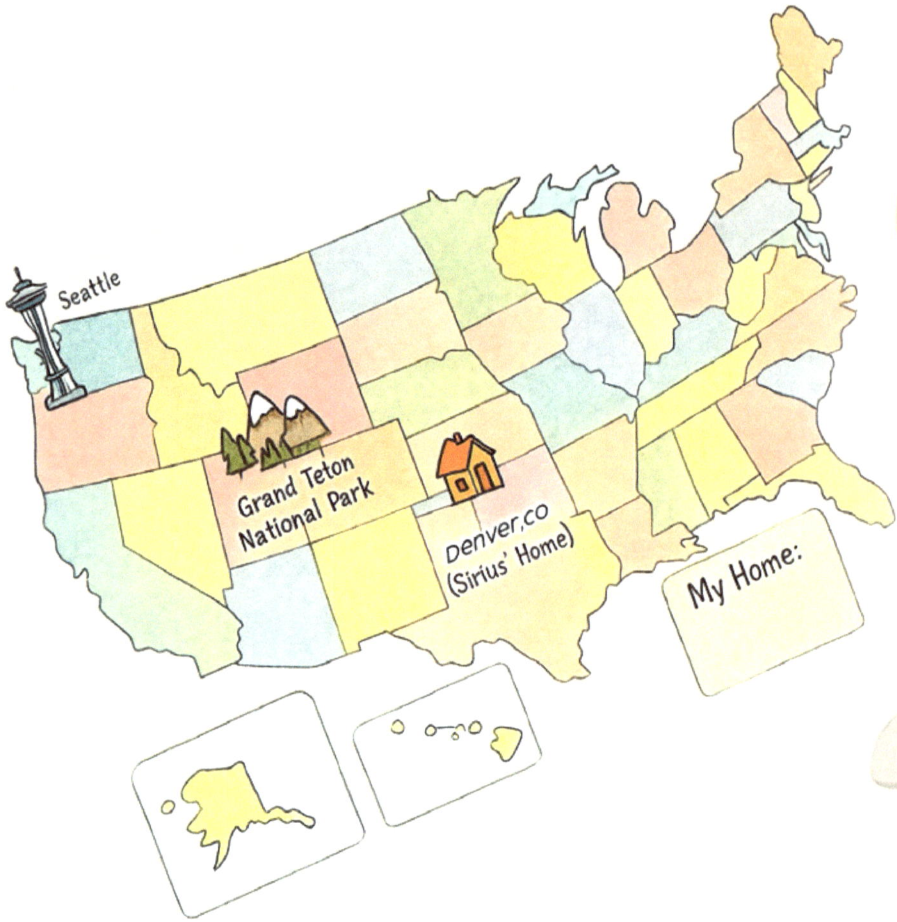
Seattle
Grand Teton
National Park
Denver,co
(Sirius' Home)
My Home:

EXPLORE THE UNITED STATES WITH SIRIUS!
Activity: Locate These Places on the Map

This is the map of the United States of America. Use it to identify the states where the following places are located:

Grand Teton National Park - Wyoming

Golden, Colorado

Seattle, Washington

Your Home - Mark where you live on the map!

# Spot & name the images

# Glossary

## Bridge

A structure built to span a physic obstacle, like water or a valley.

## Champion

A winner or someone who does something really well.

## Evergreen

A plant that keeps its green leaves all year round.

## Habitat

The natural home of an animal, plant, or other living organism.

## Hamper

A basket for dirty clothes.

## Tidy

Clean and organized.

## Trail

A path or track for walking, biking, or hiking

"Hi, I'm Sirius, and I'm a seagull."

From a gift shop shelf in Wyoming to the hearts of a loving family, Sirius's journey is full of adventure, laughter, and love. Follow him through Grand Teton National Park, the trails of Colorado, and the iconic sights of Seattle.

With humor and tenderness, Sirius the Seagull invites young readers to explore nature, celebrate family, and find joy in every adventure—complete with fun reflection activities to make the journey their own.

# About the Author

Grandma Lulu is the grandmother of a 16-year-old adolescent and a 5-year-old girl. She loves traveling, photography, and writing. Many years ago, she published two poetry books, but her creativity shifted toward children's books, inspired by spending time with her granddaughter. Their conversations cover topics like love, creativity, and education, and are full of fun, and this book captures that spirit.

www.ingramcontent.com/pod-product-compliance
Lightning Source LLC
LaVergne TN
LVHW051130210926
848482LV00001B/36